IT'S MORE THAN WISHFUL THINKING

HOPE

IT'S MORE THAN WISHFUL THINKING

HOPE

Compiled and introduced by
Amy Lyles Wilson

FRESH AIR BOOKS®
Nashville

Pages 94–95 constitute an extension of this copyright page.

Library of Congress Cataloging in Publication

Hope: it's more than wishful thinking / compiled and introduced by Amy Lyles Wilson.

   p. cm.

   ISBN: 978-1-935205-08-1

  1. Hope—Religious aspects—Christianity. I. Wilson, Amy Lyles, 1961–
   BV4638.H67 2010

241'.4—dc22   2009024289

Printed in the United States of America

Fresh Air Books is an imprint of Upper Room Books®.

Contents

INTRODUCTION
Amy Lyles Wilson

I'm hoping for a miracle," said my sister as she led me to our father's bedside in the hospital. "I'm hoping for a quick and painless exit," I responded. Two women who loved the same man, crying out for very different outcomes. And what, pray tell, did we even mean by the word *hope*? Beseeching God? Wishing for the best?

My sister and I took turns speaking to Daddy, his face partially obscured by an oxygen mask and his brain all but obliterated by a cerebral hemorrhage. If he could hear us, surely he was receiving conflicting messages. I am glad my father was the kind of man who always knew his own mind. Daddy did not survive the stroke, dying some twenty-four hours after having collapsed in a restaurant.

Even though much talk about "hope" in Christian circles revolves around the concept of the afterlife, the authors in this collection invite us to consider hope as an integral part of our *living*, not just our dying.

The hope of the faithful, we are reminded, is about much more than optimism. Hope allows humans to dream and to move forward, yes; but not as grinning, hapless fools unaware of the risks inherent in everyday life. Instead, hope informs the way we view reality. It does not encourage us to *ignore* reality. Hope accompanies us toward our next goal, ready and willing to shore us up but not allowing us to fly so high that we forget to check our parachute.

Of course, it's easy to feel hopeful when things are going our way; when the boss is happy and the children are behaving; when you feel God is smiling on you. Anyone can hope for continued sunshine on a day without clouds. But for Christians, hope empowers us to trust that we'll survive the days that are dark. Hope is not only about planning for the future, although it is that. It is also about remembering the past and reminding ourselves that just as God has been with us before, so shall God remain, whether or not our "hopes" are met to our satisfaction.

The authors in this collection, theologians and laypeople alike, invite us to respect hope as a cornerstone of faith. We would do well to rely on that promise the next time we find ourselves at the bedside of someone we love.

ALL THERE IS
Michael Downey

Stark and spare. No other words describe that room, and her. A shaft of November's afternoon light kissed the dark hardwood floor, and her. Strands of silver hair rolled up in a bun shook loose and dropped to her shoulder, hinting of girlish youth long since spent. Early days in a cloister were a faraway memory; monastic life once embraced in her native Belgium had long since been put behind. She had opted instead to be a hermit in the city, with little support from others.

It was in her second-floor apartment-become-hermitage, dedicated to Our Lady, that I would visit her in the room with a watery shine. Not often, but at the critical points.

I never saw her put a morsel to her lips. Only tea. No milk. No honey. No sugar. She looked attentively, listened long and lovingly. Around her neck a wooden cross hung from a thin black cord. It now lies at my bedside.

Graceful hands rested in her lap, folded in reverence unless she needed to make a point. Then she would raise a long and graceful forefinger as she made herself clear. On its way back to her lap, that forefinger would tuck drooping strands of silver behind her ear. She knew what she was talking about. Her voice was deep, her English still strongly laced with a Flemish accent. What she spoke of was God, and not much else.

Her frame never rested against the back of the chair. Her knees were locked nun-like. Behind her were a few photos of family members and friends. Miniature paintings and knickknacks dotted the walls. Whenever they could be had, there would be a few wildflowers in a handcrafted vase on a desk astonishing in its tidiness. Precision. Such order! My mind would wander to the Flemish Masters, with their eye for detail, awed by such reverence for the small touch in them, and in her.

The room was wrapped with bookshelves waist-high. Though arranged in categories, and then shelved alphabetically by author, it seemed rather more that the books were arranged by color and size. So neat. On each visit she would greet me at the door at the top of the stairs. Before entering the room, she led me to her small chapel. There we stood for five minutes, perhaps ten, in silent prayer before the reserved sacrament of the Eucharist. Then we went to the room, stark and spare. Indeed, at times it seemed that there was nothing in it but her.

That January was a wintry season of spirit for me. Christmas had come and gone. In a time of giving and receiving, there had been too many losses. Aside from the period following the death of my father, this seemed to be the most difficult stretch of my life. She had entered a period of deeper solitude—six weeks without contact or conversation with anyone on the outside. Reluctantly, I wrote her a note telling her I needed to see her, and left it at the hermitage door.

Her greeting was gracious and gentle, without a hint of annoyance. After the brief time together in her chapel, she pointed to the room: "You know the way." Not even a sliver of light shone from the January sun that Wednesday afternoon. Darkness came early. There seemed no light anywhere but her own.

"What happens when what you once believed no longer seems believable?" "What happens when what you have staked your life on no longer seems reliable?" "Faith says yes, and all our hope is anchored in what we have affirmed, what we have said yes to. What happens to hope, to our sense of future, when we can believe no longer?" "Can you have hope, hope in God, when faith in God is gone?" The questions poured out from the very heart of me. Indeed it seemed that I had lost everything, even and especially my most deeply cherished and firmly held convictions about God.

The room was shrouded in darkness. Yet there was enough light for me to look on her as the words came: "When you can no longer believe, that's precisely when hope begins."

Spring came, followed by an early summer. The pain in her lower back and abdomen grew worse. She was taken to the hospital, and then returned to the hermitage. Within the year she would be gone from us, taken by cancer of the stomach. She refused chemotherapy and radiation. She wanted to die in solidarity with the poor who cannot afford such medical treatment, and in a spirit of the monastic asceticism she had embraced as a girl in Belgium, a spirit to which she remained faithful as a hermit in the city. Hers was an excruciating diminishment, dying, and death. Everything was taken from her. And she was overtaken by darkness. Utter darkness. When the life seemed to have gone out of her, she would perk up to tell those near her what she had been up to during the long months of her dying. Her voice was parched and throaty, but the words were clear and, yes, precise: "Praying for the whole world."

That is what I try to do when I reach for her cross at my bedside. Holding it, my small heart is opened, if only for a moment, by the wideness of God's mercy. It is then that I remember Cecilia Wilms, religious hermit, who in her living and her dying never stopped clinging to Christ, as I do now. Yes, she held him, never letting go in faith, in love, but more, in hope.

The question about the relation of hope to faith and to love that brought me face-to-face with a hermit who knew the ways of God was not an abstract theological concern. It was something I had been carrying in my bones for several years. The question was born in the ache of absence, amidst my own losses: a father much too young to die, a beloved grandmother whose body outlived her mind by nearly twenty years, a cousin left to die of a drug overdose while his buddies slept in the same room of a crack house near our childhood home. It also was fed by the losses and tragedies of so many friends and family members, profound experiences of darkness from which emerged a bold question mark in the face of so much once believed, so much on which they had staked their lives.

Alongside my own sense of loss, and the losses of those dear to me, my attention turned with increasing frequency to the number of adolescents and impoverished people bereft of hope. I was staggered by the number of people diagnosed with clinical depression. Carrying my own losses and those of so many others, and aware of so many in our culture who seem overwhelmed by darkness, I was driven to hope. Or at least to wonder about loss and hope, about the darkness of spirit now more commonly called depression, and about the kind of hope that seems in short supply in our dark age.

What I have come to see is that there is nothing more important to human beings than hope. Certainly in our own day, many people live without explicitly religious faith. And evidence of loveless lives is tragically abundant. But people usually do not survive long without hope. They cannot, because hope is the very heart of a human being.

Oddly, though hope is so crucial to us, very little has been written about it. In comparison to faith and love, hope has been given little attention in the traditions of Christian theology and spirituality. But in our times isn't hope most important? And the most necessary? And the rarest? We live in a profoundly disruptive and disorienting age.

On every street, behind every other door, lives someone who is deeply disheartened, if not actually despairing. This may be brought on by the awareness of massive and meaningless death, the randomness of violence, the onset of early illness, the loss of a loved one, or job, or sense of meaning and value. Or by the loss of cherished and heretofore reliable ways of thinking and speaking of God. Indeed, even by the loss of faith in God. But this loss too can beckon us to deeper levels of openness to hope, the kind of hope that is absolutely and altogether gift. What exactly is this gift of hope?

Hope lies at the core of all human initiative. It looks to the coming of the new, the never-before-thought-of, the unheard-of, the undreamed-of. Hope is a pregnant, many-layered concept. We can distinguish in it different shades of meaning. We can distinguish between the kind of hope we have for good weather, the cheeriness of spirit expressed in the now commonplace "Hope you have a nice day," and something much deeper: the wholehearted anticipation of a desired good. In the deepest sense, hope moves us to a new perspective, enabling us to see the present and all its possibilities for success in light of some future good, which we realize can only come as gift. The more difficult the circumstances in which we demonstrate hope, the deeper is the hope. Hope is precisely what we have when we do not have something. Hope is not the same thing as optimism that things will go our way, or turn out well. It is rather the certainty that something makes sense, is worth the cost, regardless of how it might turn out. Hope is a sense of what might yet be. It strains ahead, seeking a way behind and beyond every obstacle.

It is not uncommon to find that what we have put our energies into (indeed what we have staked our life on) is unreliable, and that what we have affirmed in faith is no longer believable. What then is our reason for hope? Can we continue in such circumstances? It is precisely when faith crumbles and love grows dim that hope really begins; it is in the wonder and weakness of our faith that we find its real meaning. Hope is the willingness not to give up precisely when we draw no consolation from faith. It doesn't try to determine how God's ways will be shown, but remains open to new and astonishing manifestations of the divine presence. Hope is the retrieval of possibilities that come as gift. It allows something to come into life that is not self-generated. . . .

When faith in the God of our clutching and striving crumbles, there finally may be enough emptiness in us to receive what is not self-generated. When love's fire grows dim, and we stand in the dark, there finally may be a place in us to be filled with light other than our own, and by it come to know that there is neither the need to run nor the possibility of hiding. It is in this emptiness and stillness—the room in us all stark and spare—that hope begins.

GOD REMAINS
Miriam Thérèse Winter

Helper of all who are helpless,
we call on you in times of stress
and in times of devastation.
Pick up the broken pieces
of our hearts, our homes, our history
and restore them to the way they were,
or give us the means of starting over
when everything seems lost.
O God, our help in ages past,
we place all our hope in you.

LEARNING FROM THE LANDSCAPE
Robbie Clifton Pinter

Teaching requires hope. After the events of September 11, I wondered how I could have enough hope to believe that literature mattered. In the aftermath of that horrible day, Emily Dickinson's poem "A certain Slant of light" has helped me recover that hope. These words remind me of the other reality that I don't always acknowledge, the soul-filled reality where "the Landscape listens" and "Shadows hold their breath"—hoping, always hoping, for a sign, "a certain Slant of light." Now, still stinging from the realization of what can happen, I look for hope in unlikely places. Maybe we're called to search for and hear a world that is *in* this one, but not *of* it.

Such a search doesn't always make sense. Thank goodness. People need more than the ability to make sense in searching for hope. They need to believe in something more than what they can only see and hear. Within the heft, the heaviness of our lives, we can be like the landscape, looking for the slant of light that will illuminate a world that's different from the one we normally see and touch. That light brings us to the edge of understanding our worlds and gives us the courage not to understand. We have hope in what we don't see, we have faith in what we can't hear, and we keep looking and listening for the reality beyond the reality, the one we can only see when we are fully alive in our everyday worlds.

Nature offers one slant of light, suggesting a transcendent world for which many hold their breath. One spring day, as I stood on the edge of a nature preserve near my home, I listened to my friend say, "I believe the Holy Spirit is as real as the trees on the other side of the lake." We stared at the trees in silence, feeling their green dew in our own breathing. The same life in the landscape was in us. We listened with it, touching its sacred center.

Teaching offers another slant of light. In teaching, I can sometimes see students listening to their lives in such a way that they witness their own sacred centers. I once asked a student to connect one poem, play, or story with her own life. She chose *A Doll's House*, by Henrik Ibsen, focusing on the part where the main character leaves her husband to establish an identity for herself. The student reported that the play had helped her see a different reason for her mother's leaving the family when she was two. She had always thought that her mother had left because her mother was a bad person—a deserter—or worse, that her mother left because she herself was an unworthy child. Through the grace of truly hearing, the student was able to reach back through her life and see in a way she never had before. She saw her life with new eyes, and the shadows held their breath.

Listening and looking for the transcendent through daily-life events provides a way for action to grow through the fears. This attentiveness is not simply paying attention, hearing the words right, or reading something with an open attitude, although it is those things. It is more like the attentive openness that Thich Nhat Hanh, Buddhist Zen master, calls "mindfulness." Mindfulness is a kind of bodily listening that opens up both the one who speaks and the one who listens so that each can fully hear the other. Listening and seeing through the ordinary changes not only the individual but also the community.

When we listen to our own hearts, our own sacred center, we are sometimes called to act in ways that may seem foolish by the world's standards. Gandhi led hunger strikes in India and South Africa to challenge the British colonial rule and its system that implied that race determined a person's worth. In a similar David-versus-Goliath setting, a group of Nigerian women occupied an oil refinery in their village and would not let any oil leave the plant until their demands were at least heard. The women, whose only leverage was their bodies, physically blocked planes from landing and taking off until the company's representatives met with them and listened to their demands for electricity for their tin-roof shacks and jobs for their sons. Some visionaries can see the outline of another world, a better world, even through the brokenness of this one.

Connecting to our center within, whether through nature, other people, or literature, is a visceral, bodily experience. When it happens, we know it with our whole bodies, just like Emily Dickinson, who noticed a shaft of light and described it in a way that speaks to the sacred center of many of her readers. We have been there. Deep inside, we know what she means, that we have witnessed the lights that were supposed to be hope but were not. We have seen buildings fall that should not have fallen, watched people die who were not supposed to die, and witnessed dreams fade that were supposedly strong enough to last a lifetime. No wonder the shadows hold their breath. They're looking and listening for a world they cannot see or hear at first glance, but which is, nonetheless, incarnate all around us. And when it comes, we would all do well, like the landscape, to hold our breath.

STANDING FIRM
Parker J. Palmer

We have places of fear inside of us, but we have other places as well—places with names like trust and hope and faith. We can choose to lead from one of *those* places, to stand on ground that is not riddled with the fault lines of fear, to move toward others from a place of promise instead of anxiety. As we stand in one of those places, fear may remain close at hand and our spirits may still tremble. But now we stand on ground that will support us, ground from which we can lead others toward a more trustworthy, more hopeful, more faithful way of being in the world.

HARBINGERS TO HUMANKIND
E. Glenn Hinson

There is much needless and senseless suffering in our world today, and it is right to do everything in our power to eliminate it. [Quaker theologian] Thomas Kelly called suffering a "fruit of holy obedience." Freshly returned from Europe as it plunged into the Second World War, he wrote:

> The heart is stretched through suffering, and enlarged. But O the agony of the enlarging of the heart, that one may be prepared to enter into the anguish of others! Yet the way of holy obedience leads out from the heart of God and extends through the Valley of the Shadow.[1]

We are to be fellow sufferers and harbingers of hope to humankind.

In *The Agony and the Ecstasy* Irving Stone recounts the story of Michelangelo's sculpting of one of his most famous statues. Sculptors came from all over Europe to take part in a sculpting contest. The stone to be sculpted was a giant marble slab seventeen feet high. As the artists filed by to view the stone, however, one by one they shook their heads in dismay, for that stone was marred in vital places by nicks, pits, and gouges. Michelangelo, the greatest of the world's great sculptors, paused longer than the others, and he saw taking shape in his mind's eye a form. From that marble column he carved his "David."

Humanity is like that marble column. Human life is like it. Your life and my life are like it. They have been marred in vital places. God is seeking fellow sufferers who will pause longer than others and look more deeply than others. God is looking for some who can be harbingers of hope to humankind.

A DEFINITION OF HOPE
The Upper Room Dictionary
of Christian Spiritual Formation

HOPE. A stance of confidence that just as God has been faithful in the past, God will also provide for the future. Christians live in the present with a distinct orientation toward the future. . . .

Hope is a necessary dimension of Christian faith in this life and in the life to come. A portion of our hope must be in this life. . . . But a portion of our hope must be placed in the life to come, for justice, peace, and righteousness are not always realized in the human experience.

We claim God's gift of hope in many ways: in reading the scriptures, in praying for the kingdom, in receiving Holy Communion (a foretaste of the messianic banquet), and in singing hymns from different Christian traditions. Ultimately hope is grounded in the experience of Easter and in the presence of the risen Lord in the ongoing life of the church.

ALWAYS THERE IS GOD
Diana C. Derringer

There are times in our lives when
the pain is so great,
the sorrow so intense,
the confusion so overwhelming
that we think we cannot possibly continue.

Yet, in those very moments
God's love can be so real,
God's presence so unmistakable,
and God's peace so calming.

God offers to wrap us
in arms of peace,
fill us with everlasting joy,
and shower us with unconditional love.

God is simply waiting for us
to ask God to enter our lives,
to forgive us our failures,
and to give us hope.

Our difficulties may remain,
but we no longer have to carry them alone.
God will not leave.
God will not fail.
God is ever-present God.

MORE THAN OPTIMISM
Doris Donnelly

For many years, hope has suffered the fate of a middle child. On either side of her are her two more popular sisters, faith and charity, leaving hope invisible, or ignored, and frequently misunderstood. . . .

Hope is not wishy-washy, nor is she comfortable with doubt. A good example of this first misconception about hope happens in ordinary, daily conversation. Someone asks, "Is your telephone working?" And another answers, "I hope so." The response is, in a sense, the opposite of confidence and security. In fact, "I hope so" sounds like a wish tinged with lots of doubt. What the responder seems to be saying is "I'm not sure; maybe . . . but maybe not." And either of these responses falls short of the biblical understanding of hope that doesn't doubt even though at the same time it never sees the thing it hopes for.

Second, many people use *hope* when they really mean *hopelessness*. So they say things like "Well, there's nothing left for us to do but hope" that in translation mean "We might as well give up; it's hopeless."

Third, there are those who speak of hope in situations not worthy of hope's power: "I hope to win the lottery." "I hope she calls by noon." "I hope I can get a reservation." These are frivolous uses of hope. Hope's range of activity exceeds all such puny and sometimes inappropriate desires. The hope the Bible talks about is far more serious. For example, the apostle Paul insists on the universality of hope in everything we do. It could not be more obvious for him: After the resurrection of Jesus, we actually live by hope—*we live by it*—so that every fiber of our being is bound up with it. This passionate acknowledgment gets at the truth that only one person can fulfill our hope for healing and salvation—and that is Jesus Christ. This is hope on a grand scale, and its promises are likewise proportionately large.

A fourth and perhaps most common way that hope is misunderstood is as optimism. Often the terms are used interchangeably, and we frequently picture the upbeat optimist as a person of hope. But there may be nothing further from the truth than that. Optimism is a surface quality, a mind-set that sees something positive in all situations—even hopeless ones. It is a Pollyannaish attitude that often refuses to acknowledge illness, hurt, woundedness, sin, tragedy, and despair. "Cheer up," the optimist tells us, "things are sure to get better tomorrow!" Hope, on the other hand, is not an attitude but a virtue that faces reality head-on, reads situations often as bad going to worse—things very well might not get better tomorrow!—and knows that no matter how reality presents itself, ultimately all shall be well.

OUR DESPAIRING HOPE
Walter Brueggemann

Among us are shrivelled women
>who in despair do not eat,
>who in powerlessness weep downcast,
>whose lips tremble, and
>who barely dare ask otherwise.
>We in our compassion and sensitivity
>stand alongside those shrivelled women,
>who in despair do not eat,
>who in powerlessness weep downcast,
>whose lips tremble, and
>who barely dare ask otherwise.
Down deep in all candor we ourselves
>are among those shrivelled women;
>we also in despair do not eat,
>we also in powerlessness weep downcast,

we also have lips that tremble, and

we also barely dare ask otherwise.

They wait . . .

We wait alongside them . . .

We wait.

And you . . . sometimes . . . speak shalom and the world is made new.

This day in our despairing hope,

grant that we, along with all shrivelled women,

may—before sundown—eat and praise and depart in peace.

For now, we wait. Amen.

A NEW UNDERSTANDING
Joan D. Chittister

H ope," the fantasy writer[s] Margaret Weis [and Tracy Hickman] wrote, "is the denial of reality."[1]

I completely disagree.

Reality is the only thing we have that can possibly nourish hope. Hope is not based on the ability to fabricate a better future; it is grounded in the ability to remember with new understanding an equally difficult past—either our own or someone else's. The fact is that our memories are the seedbed of our hope. They are the only things we have that prove to us that whatever it was we ever before thought would crush us to the grave, would trample our spirits into perpetual dust, would fell us in our tracks, had actually been survived. And if that is true, then whatever we are wrestling with now can also be surmounted.

Hope lies in the memory of God's previous goodness to us in a world that is both bountiful and harsh. The God who created this world loves it and us in it, but at the price of our own effort, at the cost of our own craving for more of the vision, more of the depth, more of the truth of the life. The God who made this world has blessed it with good things, yes—but all of them take working at: coconuts need to be cracked, soil needs to be tilled, mountains need to be climbed, water needs to be conserved. God does not do this for us. God simply companions us as we go. God has given us in this unfinished world a glimpse of eternity and walks with us through here to there, giving us possibility, giving us hope.

The proofs of eternal rebirth are everywhere. Spring comes every year. Dawn comes every morning. Love happens out of hate. Birth absorbs the pain of death. And people everywhere look to Nirvana, to enlightenment, to reincarnation, to resurrection in the hope of eternal renewal. To the Christian, both the crucifixion and the resurrection of Jesus we see as proof of God's will for the world, and in the Paschal Mystery the demonstration of the cycle of struggle.

It is true that the Jesus who lives in us died but did not die. But just as true is the fact that we have all known resurrection in our own lives as well. We have been crucified, each of us, one way or another, and been raised up again. What had been bad for us at the time, we now see, was in the end an invitation to rise to new life. The invitation was to a road, we now admit, which we would never have taken ourselves if we had not been forced to travel it. Looking back we know now that this hard road was really the journey that brought us at least one step closer to wholeness in a world in which wholeness can never exist. It may be precisely because we lust after some kind of mythical wholeness that we fail to see the life-giving truths that come to us one byway, one fragment at a time.

Hope is not some kind of delusional optimism to be resorted to because we simply cannot face the hard facts that threaten to swamp our hearts. People do die and leave us. Friends do leave and desert us. Businesses do crumble and destroy us financially. Loves do dry up and disappear. Desires do come to dust. Careers do come to ruin. Disease does debilitate us. Evil does exist. But through it all, hope remains, nevertheless, a choice.

Hope rides on the decision either to believe that God stands on this dark road waiting to walk with us toward new light again or to despair of the fact that God who is faithful is eternally faithful and will sustain us in our darkness one more time. We can begin to build a new life when death comes. We can reach out to make friends with others rather than curl up, hurt and angry, waiting for someone to come to us. We can allow ourselves to love again, knowing now that love is a prize that comes in many shapes and forms. We can allow ourselves to cultivate new joys, new interests. We can take the experiences of the past and use them to mine a new life lode. We can give ourselves over to resisting what must be resisted whether we ever live to see it expelled or not. We can let go of a finished present so that what is about to happen in the future can begin. We can decide to go through life with open hands rather than to trap ourselves inside a heart closed to everything but the past.

Hope and despair are not opposites. They are cut from the very same cloth, made from the very same material, shaped from the very same circumstances. Every life finds itself forced to choose one from the other, one day at a time, one circumstance after another. The sunflower, that plant which in shadow turns its head relentlessly toward the sun, is the patron saint of those in despair. When darkness descends on the soul, it is time, like the sunflower, to go looking for whatever good thing in life there is that can bring us comfort. Then we need music and hobbies and friends and fun and new thought—not alcohol and wild nights and immersion in the pain that is killing us. The worst thing is to dull rather than displace the pain with the kind of joy or comfort that makes us new. "Give light," Erasmus wrote, "and the darkness will disappear of itself." . . .

Despair colors the way we look at things, makes us suspicious of the future, makes us negative about the present. Most of all, despair leads us to ignore the very possibilities that could save us, or worse, leads us to want to hurt as we have been hurt ourselves.

Hope, on the other hand, takes life on its own terms, knows that whatever happens God lives in it, and expects that, whatever its twists and turns, it will ultimately yield its good to those who live it consciously, to those who live it to the hilt.

When tragedy strikes, when trouble comes, when life disappoints us, we stand at the crossroads between hope and despair, torn and hurting. Despair cements us in the present. Hope sends us dancing around dark corners trusting in a tomorrow we cannot see because of the multiple pasts of life which we cannot forget. Despair says that there is no place to go but here.

When I say that I am in despair, I am really saying that I have given up on God. Despair says that I am God and if I can't do anything about this situation, then nothing and nobody can.

Despair is the affliction of the small-minded who have not so much lost their faith as they have lost their memory. Hope says, remember where you have been before and know that God is waiting for you someplace else now, to go on again to something new.

Life is not one road. It is many roads, the walking of which provides the raw material out of which we find hope in the midst of despair. Every dimension of the process of struggle is a call to draw from a well of new understandings. It is in these understandings that hope dwells. It is that wisdom that carries us beyond the dark night of struggle to the dawn of new wisdom and new strength.

NOTORIOUS HOPE
Rueben P. Job

As Christians we live by faith in God, and we carry within us the notorious hope that a life of faithfulness is indeed the best way to live. Our hope is that fidelity and faithfulness will result in a holy life and the comforting companionship of Jesus Christ. The rewards of peace and assurance of continued companionship with God in the life to come belong to every faithful Christian.

We hope for that which we do not see. The reward of holy living today is merely a hope for tomorrow. The rewards of peace and assurance may be ours today, but they are only a hope for tomorrow. The companionship of Jesus Christ is experienced today but is only a hope for tomorrow. The promise that this ordinary life can be invested in the extraordinary reign of God today and tomorrow is the hope that encourages us to do what we can where we are to make God's will known and real.

When disease, disaster, death, or triumph strike, we are filled with hope because our ultimate trust is in God. Our worlds and wealth may crumble; disease and disaster may lay hold on what and whom we value; but followers of the Christian way continue to be hopeful. We hold onto hope because we are filled with faith that God is able to consummate the promise made to redeem and transform all who turn their lives toward God.

THE NECESSITY OF PATIENCE
Stanley Hauerwas

Hope without patience results in the illusion of optimism or, more terrifying, the desperation of fanaticism. The hope necessary to initiate us into the adventure must be schooled by patience if the adventure is to be sustained. Through patience we learn to continue to hope even though our hope seems to offer little chance of fulfillment. . . . Yet patience equally requires hope, for without hope patience too easily accepts the world and the self for what it is rather than what it can or should be.

AGAINST ALL HOPE
Roberto Escamilla

Frequently we live in a condition of "in between." We are always between success and failure; between enthusiasm and boredom; between despair and hope—hope and despair—despair and hope.

The truth is, we need to keep alive the dialectic between hope and despair. It is precisely as a result of this dialectic tension that we are able to go beyond hope and despair.

There are moments in the life of every human being when all hopes seem to have died like the leaves of the trees in autumn. Sometimes, it is impossible to hide the sadness that is in the depth of our souls.

Despair is like a tragic captivity that sometimes leads us very close to the abyss, and only a miracle can keep us from falling into it. Despair is agony—the agony of not finding a solution to our dilemma of wondering with uncertainty about the world. . . .

Sometimes hope comes about as the tolling of the bells heard in the midst of the business of life, or as a small light that shines forth in the horizon when there is no other. It is in the midst of misfortune that the character and endurance of a person are manifested.

DON'T LOOK BACK
Leigh McLeroy

My favorite form of exercise is a brisk early morning walk through my neighborhood—sometimes before the sun comes up. I walk east so that I can watch the horizon go from dark to light in colors nearly impossible to describe, and I almost always see something new.

On a heavy-garbage pickup day, I spotted something abandoned on the curb of a favorite tree-lined street. As I got closer I could see that it was an exercise machine—left lying on its side like a capsized metal cricket, waiting for the trashmen to rumble down the block and toss it in their truck.

I suppose it's not terribly unusual to abandon an exercise machine, or an exercise program. I've abandoned a few in my time. But in January (and it was) most of us are purchasing such machines or beginning such programs, not leaving them behind. In January, most of us still have hope in our own resourcefulness, our own determination, our own power to move mountains—even if the mountain is us! In January we're optimistic that we have the right mind-set to achieve our targeted goals, regardless of past failures. So why did my neighbor leave his exerciser on the curb two weeks into a brand-new year?

As I walked, I imagined all kinds of scenarios. Maybe he bought the machine *last* January, and it hadn't had the hoped-for results—or it had, and he was done with all the effort. (Big mistake.) Maybe he'd begun another program or acquired a better machine. Or maybe he overestimated his own dedication and simply failed to follow through.

The abandoned machine pointed to one of two things: either its former owner had no hope, or he had a new hope.

In Christ we aren't given a mulligan—we're given new hope. We can begin again—it's true. But we no longer hope in our own goodness, or in God's willingness to overlook our shortcomings, or judge us favorably in light of someone else whose performance we deem even less worthy than our own. We don't hope in our own power to effect change, or to manage the circumstances of our lives.

Instead we have a new and living hope: we have a Savior who defeated death itself, and who lives to tell.

This new hope of ours is attached to something solid, immovable, and certain. It's an anchor, this hope. And its heavy end rests in a place where we've never been before but one day will.

They say the road to hell is paved with good intentions. I'm beginning to wonder if the road to heaven isn't littered with abandoned ones: left-behind intentions that, like the exerciser a few blocks over, might just be a sign that a new and better hope has taken up residence.

Everything that is done in the world
is done by hope.[1]

—MARTIN LUTHER

❧

IT'S THAT GOOD
Sam Davidson

Hope, like most intangible nouns, tries its best to make sense to us in the form of comparisons. The writer of Hebrews compares it to faith, which is a "vision of things not seen." Others may tell you it's persevering when everyone around you tells you to quit. It's the flower that sprouts up in a sidewalk crack or the child who faithfully writes Santa, asking for a shiny bicycle.

And while these definitions and images may work for some of us, they usually fall short in a world of jobs, bills, families, and technology. They seem too quaint in a world of war, death, disease, injustice, and poverty. Flowers in sidewalks and kids' wish lists just don't cut it for a lot of us.

To me, hope is driving to a job you hate, to work too long of a shift in order to get paid too little money. You keep doing it because you believe that there's more than this.

That's what hope is—it's the belief that something else is on the horizon, something better is waiting for you; and even if you're not sure what it is, you're willing to wait for it. Because it will be *that* good.

We hope for a lot of things. We hope it won't rain tomorrow. We hope our team wins tonight. We hope that our kids will live in a more peaceful world and that they'll be productive members of society.

Those hopes are hardly idle, but they come across our lips as less than exciting. In those contexts, we do little to see that those hopes of ours become reality. It's a passive hope. Or maybe it's more like wishful thinking. This kind of hope, while good and comforting, ultimately does little for our soul. It's very easy to passively, quietly, and even lazily hope. It's nothing more than uttering a phrase or having a thought.

Active hope—hope that demands we do something—well, that's hard. Active hope requires work, which means we have to get our hands dirty, sweat a little bit, get uncomfortable and maybe even cry, bleed, or run out of breath. That's a hope that won't let us stay in bed while the clock ticks and the world marches on.

It's a hope that makes us open our wallets and support the nonprofit that is doing so much for orphans. It's a hope that sends us to another neighborhood to pick up a saw or hammer so someone we've never met can have a roof over her head. It's a hope that makes us question our own lifestyle when so many in the world subsist on what we spend for a latte. It's a hope that hurts.

Deep down, that's the hope that we really want. It's a hope that is deeper than diet pills and more like exercise. Sure, we love the easy way out, but lasting change and tangible hope happen when we put skin in the game and invest our very selves in creating a better world, and not just clicking our heels until it magically appears.

Convenient hope is easy to come by, and everyone sells it. Real hope is rare—so rare that we'll mortgage our current lifestyle to be able to own it.

How then can you find this real hope? *By giving it away.*

When we offer hope to someone else, we'll see it return to us. Offering hope to someone rarely requires any money. It will, however, demand our energy; our creativity; our time, attention, and presence. When we see that someone has grasped the hope that we've offered in the form of a conversation, a friendship, or a favor, we'll receive some ourselves. And that just might be enough to get us down the road a bit.

Don't be fooled if hope is offered to you in a nicely packaged form, like some sort of latest cellular phone or video game. Cleverly branded hope may not be much once you really need it. That's how I think about a lot of technology.

While I'm by no means an early adopter of the newest and snazziest, I'm earlier than some. I've never waited in line to buy the first of anything. Waiting a few months (or even years) before buying something technological doesn't put me on the cutting edge, but it has saved me some headaches. Whenever I purchase a new digital gadget, I usually try to get one that will *work* for me—something that will make me more productive, stay in better touch, or even have a competitive advantage in my work. So, even though I'm never first in line, I still have every bit as much hope as those people who camped out overnight just to own that same piece of equipment six months before me.

I suggest that something "religious" is happening in this scenario. The world over, people are pinning their hopes of community, communication, and connectivity on wires and microprocessors. When I blog, I hope that people will hear my story. When I e-mail a friend, I hope that we'll strengthen our relationship. When I make a phone call, I hope I can create value for my company.

Of course, the minute our networks and connections fail, we feel stranded in a sea of despair. When we can't e-mail or message people, find information quickly, or post a funny picture online, what do we have to live for?

I believe that our world needs more hope than our technological progress could ever provide. Rarely will you find much hope in newspaper headlines. Most of the time, you won't find it in the mail. Every once in a while, you may find some at church. Ideally, your friends and family are happy to supply you with some.

It's easy to run out of hope. That's why we need more. The hope of a certain career path can be dashed instantly with a call to meet the boss in her office. The hope of an elite education can disappear with the opening of an envelope. And the hope of healthy golden years vanishes when the doctor shares the test results.

Hoping is more than wishful thinking. It's the very deepest longing of our soul. We long for hope like our dry mouth craves drink. And when we get it, even just a little bit, it radically alters the course of our day—and our lives.

It was hope that led us to choosing one college over the other. And because of that, our career path and lifelong friendships unfolded in a drastically different way than they would have had we attended school elsewhere. It was hope that determined who we voted for, who we asked to the dance, and who we dreamed our children would marry.

Hope makes us walk in certain restaurants, excited about the meal we're about to order. Hope makes us go to the mall to buy a new shirt so that we'll be noticed and in style. Hope sends us time and again to the driving range in anticipation that the next round of golf will be a few strokes better. Hope sends us to the hospital to keep vigil or speak with doctors so that the best decisions can be made and the favorable outcomes can be achieved.

Hope happens every time a mother talks to her child in the womb, every time a teacher believes a kid can learn, and every time a volunteer serves a meal. Hope happens every time an individual walks into a voting booth, listens to a friend's lament, or cooks dinner for the grieving.

Indeed, hope is alive in every metropolis and hamlet, even if we haven't called it that. When we sit across the dinner table from someone, we hope that the conversation and time spent together over a meal will strengthen a relationship and make us happier. When we decide to donate the change in our pockets to the man with a cardboard sign near the off-ramp of the interstate, we hope that those coins will get him what he's looking for. And when we hop on a plane to spend a week somewhere on a beach, we hope that we'll be reminded of why we work our jobs, why we love our families, and why it may not get any better than this.

Why then, are so many people still in need of hope?

I think it's because not many people are offering the real thing. Lots of people have been selling hope and have made out like bandits. Whether it's a diet pill, a new cell phone, a kitchen gadget, or a cleaning supply, it's all hawked in a way that for one low fee, you can have a better, more productive, or more fulfilled life. And what could be more hopeful that that?

Instead, if more people gave hope away for free, we wouldn't be so disappointed when our gadgets break and our technologies fail. Our deepest hopes would never be placed in what can be found on a store shelf. Instead, we'd have hope in community, humanity, and a better tomorrow.

The question remains: How will you offer hope to someone today? Maybe you have nothing to give but your time, nothing to leverage but your ears and attention, and nothing to gain but some hope for yourself.

And maybe that's the secret of hope—once we offer it, we'll find it.

ANOTHER TOMORROW
Andrew Greeley

The hopeful person, then, is one who survives because he believes in survival; he lives because he believes in life; and he celebrates because he believes he has something worth celebrating. He can afford to be more tolerant of others because others are less likely to threaten him. Diversity is not a challenge to his individuality or his freedom because he knows that nothing can really destroy that which is most uniquely and essentially himself. He is perhaps not any less afraid of death; we are all afraid of death. But he is not paralyzed by that fear, he will give up and quit, anticipating death by dying psychologically and humanly long before he dies physically. The hopeful person dies only once. He lives strongly and vitally up to the point of death.

Hopefulness does not preclude discouragement, disillusion, frustration; it does preclude bitterness and cynicism. Hopefulness does not mean that we do not fall; but it does mean that we get up and walk on. Hopefulness says with T. S. Eliot, "Disillusion if persisted in is the ultimate illusion." Life is not a bowl of cherries, it is not a picnic, or even a parade; it is, quite literally, a deadly serious business. It is so serious that a Christian, obsessed as he is by hope, has no choice but to laugh about it. He says with Gregory Baum that "tomorrow will be different, even if tomorrow is the day after the last day of our lives." It may well rain on today's parade, but let's see about tomorrow.

And this expectation for what tomorrow may bring is the final, most special, most distinctive aspect of the Christian "life before death." The Christian is curious, he wonders about tomorrow, he is intrigued by its possibilities and fundamentally unafraid of its terrors. John Shea has written that the best way a Christian can prepare for death is to develop a healthy capacity for surprise. It seems to me that that is the best description of the Christian life I have ever read. We are engaged in the business of developing our capacity for surprise. No matter how worn or weary or battered or frustrated or tired we may be, we still have an ability to wonder; we are still open, curious, expectant, waiting to be surprised. What will be around that next corner? Who lurks behind that bush? What is that Cheshire cat smile that just vanished in the leaves of yonder tree? Who is that knocking at the door? Who is messing around the garden? Who is trying to peek in through the latticework? Who is that making all the noise, leaping and bounding around over there in the hills? What's going on here? Is there some kind of conspiracy, some kind of plot? Who is the Plotter? There is something mysterious about this house. There's a Ghost in it, and he just went down the corridor. What the hell is going to happen next?

Ultimately, then, the universe is either an empty machine held together by some clever but essential brute force, or it is a haunted house spooked by playful ghosts. In the machine there is no wonder or mystery; in the haunted house there are a thousand puzzles, lots of tricks, and a surprise a minute. The best ghost stories are always comedies, so there is also a laugh a minute. Like Thomas More, we may even die laughing.

So the Christian goes to bed at night not afraid that he will wake up tomorrow to find himself dead, but curious as to what crazy fool surprise lays in store for him when he wakes up in the sometimes frightening, sometimes absurd, sometimes even vicious but always fascinating haunted house of a world.

Or, to sum up the whole Christian argument, how do we know that tomorrow will be different? Every other tomorrow we have known has been different. Why shouldn't the next one?

TURNING
Ann Conner

Water runs through high
cloud to root,
root to leaf, wind
to cloud just as now
wet with hope,
Your Spirit finds me here
dry in the dark, turning
from dust finally
to a new shoot
enfolded, still blind, yet
ready to fly.

FLING YOUR FEET TOWARD HEAVEN
Frederick Buechner

In the year 1831, it seems, this church was repaired and several new additions were made. One of them was a new steeple with a bell in it, and once it was set in place and painted, apparently, an extraordinary event took place. "When the steeple was added," Howard Mudgett writes in his history, "one agile Lyman Woodard stood on his head in the belfry with his feet toward heaven."

That's the one and only thing I've been able to find out about Lyman Woodard, whoever he was, but it is enough. I love him for doing what he did. It was a crazy thing to do. It was a risky thing to do. It ran counter to all standards of New England practicality and prudence. It stood the whole idea that you're supposed to be nothing but solemn in church on its head just like Lyman himself standing upside down on his. And it was also a magical and magnificent and Mozartian thing to do.

If the Lord is indeed our shepherd, then everything goes topsy-turvy. Losing becomes finding and crying becomes laughing. The last become first and the weak become strong. Instead of life being done in by death in the end as we always supposed, death is done in finally by life in the end. If the Lord is our host at the great feast, then the sky is the limit.

There is plenty of work to be done down here, God knows. To struggle each day to walk the paths of righteousness is no pushover, and struggle we must because just as we are fed like sheep in green pastures, we must also feed his sheep, which are each other. Jesus, our shepherd, tells us that. We must help bear each other's burdens. We must pray for each other. We must nourish each other, weep with each other, rejoice with each other. Sometimes we must just learn to let each other alone. In short, we must love each other. We must never forget that. But let us never forget Lyman Woodard either silhouetted up there against the blue Rupert sky. Let us join him in the belfry with our feet toward Heaven like his because Heaven is where we are heading. That is our faith and what better image of faith could there be? It is a little crazy. It is a little risky. It sets many a level head wagging. And it is also our richest treasure and the source of our deepest joy and highest hope.

A RISKY PROPOSITION
Martin E. Marty

Hope does not equal risk, but it always entails risk. When we hope, we may be tempted to romanticize refuges of the past. In imagination and desire we then flee from the present, the limits of which we have come to know. Hope is risky, because when the futures for which it prepares us arrive, we are so often disappointed by outcomes and by ourselves.

To minimize the risks that come along with hoping, we often fall silent and do not announce hopes. Announce them and we disappoint others whenever our desires fail to be realized. Or we delight those who get ego-satisfaction from seeing dreamers frustrated. To deal with hopes unfulfilled, the wise ones learn to ready a "Plan B," a set of goals that more nearly match the desires and realities of the mature. It becomes evident then that hope cannot be isolated from the rest of life. It needs a balance in common sense that tells us to reckon with and, where possible, savor the present.

Meanwhile, for the sake of risk, we need some solid place to stand, against which to lean, to which to return. Builders create pillars, foundations, and buttresses. For believers, when other supports give out, Christ remains the rock, solid, on which to stand. From whence to dare.

THE REAL THING
John Indermark

There is nothing very concrete about [hope],
and its use is very wishy-washy.

—Rev. Roddy Hamilton

Rev. Hamilton's words . . . do not reflect my core beliefs about hope. But I read his words and nod in sad agreement, because their implicit critique of what passes for hope is absolutely on target.

Too much that passes for hope among us is little more than wishful thinking disconnected from action taken in response. Too much that passes for hope reflects the self-centered daydreaming about what would be nice for me and mine to the exclusion of any concrete consideration for you and yours. Too much that passes for hope wants to let go and let God, even in those matters where our gracious God waits and waits for us to act. To term such hope *wishy-washy* is gentle understatement. Such a parody of hope leaves us spiritually homeless, stripped of the calling and direction so vital in biblical faith.

Such false optimisms lead us nowhere of value. They are no better, and perhaps even more deceitful, than wearying pessimisms that abandon us in despair and cynicism. Sometimes we are seduced into thinking those are the only available options. Yet the writings of Israel and of the early church bear witness to a third option: the way of hope. The deep hopes of those communities resonate in the imagery of faith as a journey toward home. As the author of Hebrews puts it: "People who speak in this way make it clear that they are seeking a homeland." Hope involves finding where and to whom we and all creation belong and then having the trust and courage to start living in that direction. . . .

. . . We walk and work, we choose and hope—*now*. In this moment, in this place. While hope keeps its eyes fixed on the future, hope also keeps feet planted firmly on the ground and hands thick in the mix of life lived now. Why? Because the journey begins here.

LIFELONG LESSON
John R. Claypool

The first step in understanding hope is to acknowledge the deep mystery that pervades all human experience, a mystery that should call forth in us a stance of genuine humility. Here we are, in a world that we did not create, surrounded by much that we neither understand nor comprehend. The Psalmist reminds us, "It is God who hath made us, and not we ourselves" (100:3), which is to say that we are radically contingent beings. After all, we did not will ourselves into this world, nor did we set in motion this incredible process of history in which we find ourselves. There is so much that makes up this existence of ours that we cannot explain, so much that we simply do not have the intellectual capacity to comprehend. Thus, the humility that is implied by saying, "We know in part and we see through a glass darkly," is actually an acceptance of the fact that mystery is the true context of our lives.

I remember vividly a glimpse into these two pathways to hopefulness given to me by a wonderful old Jewish rabbi, whom I had befriended in the turbulent 1960s. I need to confess that growing up in the southern way of life in Nashville during the 1930s and 1940s, I did not even realize that there was a racial problem in our culture. I embraced the way whites and blacks related to each other back then as an acceptable norm. However, in the fall of 1950, a man named Clarence Jordan came to the little college that I was attending, and in one week's time, he turned my perceptual world upside down and created for me what is often described as "the white man's burden." I realized that our segregated way of living was a contradiction, not only of our national ideals, but also of the heart of the gospel. From that time forward, I felt called to do what I could to achieve racial equality. All of my family's forebears were slave-owners, and this motivated me to try to be a part of the answer where I felt my kind had been part of the problem.

When I began to serve a church in Louisville, Kentucky, in 1960, I immediately aligned myself with groups that were working to heal our cultural sickness, and that is how I met this gracious old rabbi. We were an odd couple in many ways. He was in his seventies, and his family had been through the Holocaust in Eastern Europe. He knew much about the dark side of human existence while I, on the other hand, was very naive and had not yet been initiated into the fraternity of the suffering. We were working together in the civil rights movement and, one afternoon, we participated in a very tense meeting with several African American ministers. They finally stormed out in a rage, accusing us whites of having no courage, and what began as a hopeful endeavor ended in total frustration. We happened to be meeting in this rabbi's synagogue, and as I left, I said to him, "I think it is hopeless. This problem is so old, so deep, so many-faceted, there is simply no way out of it." He responded by saying, "If you have a few minutes, I would like to talk to you about what you have just said." With that, he ushered me into his study and we both sat down.

I still remember how unhurriedly he lit his pipe and disappeared for a moment in a cloud of smoke. As the smoke began to dissipate, he said, "I need to tell you something, young man. To the Jew, there is only one unforgivable sin, and that is the sin of despair." He continued, "Humanly speaking, despair is presumptuous. It is saying something about the future that we have no right to say because we have not been there yet and do not know enough. Think of the times you have been surprised in the past as you looked at a certain situation and deemed it hopeless. Then, lo and behold, forces that you did not even realize existed broke in and changed everything. We do not know enough to embrace the absolutism of despair and, theologically speaking, despair is downright heretical. If God can create the things that are from the things that are not, and even make dead things come back to life, who are we to set limits on what that kind of potency may yet do?"

CYNICS AND SAINTS
Jim Wallis

Perhaps the only people who view the world realistically are the cynics and the saints. Everybody else may be living in some kind of denial about what is really going on and how things really are. And the only difference between the cynics and the saints is the presence, power, and possibility of hope. And that, indeed, is a spiritual and religious issue. More than just a moral issue, hope is a spiritual and even religious choice. Hope is not a feeling; it is a decision. And the decision for hope is based on what you believe at the deepest levels— what your most basic convictions are about the world and what the future holds—all based on your faith. You choose hope, not as a naive wish, but as a choice, with your eyes wide open to the reality of the world—just like the cynics who have not made the decision for hope.

SUGGESTIONS FOR
MAINTAINING HOPE IN YOUR LIFE

1

Allow yourself to live fully in the present while trusting in tomorrow.

2

Don't ignore reality, but try not to let yourself become overwhelmed by it either.

3

Reflect on a problem in your life that once seemed insurmountable but has since been resolved.

4

Develop healthy strategies for getting you through the tough times.

5

Remember that hope is more than optimism and wishful thinking.

6

Reach out to someone in need, someone who has less hope than you do.

7

Work toward your goals and follow your dreams, knowing that both require action.

8

Seek professional help if you find yourself in despair.

9

Make a list of ten people who make you feel hopeful.

10

Don't give up on yourself or God.

NOTES

HARBINGERS TO HUMANKIND

1. Thomas R. Kelly, *A Testament of Devotion* (New York: Harper and Brothers, 1941), 71.

A NEW UNDERSTANDING

1. Margaret Weis and Tracy Hickman, *Dragons of Winter Night,* Dragonlance Chronicles, vol. 2 (Renton, WA: Wizards of the Coast, 2000), 15.

EVERYTHING THAT IS DONE

1. Martin Luther, *Table Talk,* no. 298, http://www.ccel.org/ccel/luther/tabletalk.txt.

Contributors

Walter Brueggemann is an American Old Testament scholar and author. He has authored more than fifty-eight books, hundreds of articles, and several commentaries.

Frederick Buechner, an ordained Presbyterian minister, is the author of more than thirty books. He has been a finalist for the National Book Award and the Pulitzer Prize.

Joan D. Chittister is a Benedictine nun and an international lecturer. Sister Joan is the founder and current executive director of Benetvision, a resource and research center for contemporary spirituality.

John R. Claypool was ordained as an Episcopal priest in 1986 and served as Rector of St. Luke's Episcopal Church in Birmingham, Alabama, for nearly fourteen years. He served as professor of homiletics at Mercer University's School of Theology in Atlanta and wrote more than ten books. He died in 2005.

Ann Conner is a reporter and editor who learned to uncover truth and to check the source. Now living in Kansas with her husband, she writes and grows to seek living water and to find it in the cross of Christ.

Sam Davidson is cofounder and president of Cool People Care. A speaker, writer, and dreamer with a few years in the nonprofit world, Sam seeks to tell the stories that need telling in order to motivate people to change the things that need changing (www.coolpeoplecare.org).

Diana C. Derringer is a retired family services clinician and adjunct professor who teaches Sunday school and works in outreach missions through her church.

Doris Donnelly is a professor of theology at John Carroll University in University Heights, Ohio.

Michael Downey, Cardinal's Theologian, Archdiocese of Los Angeles, is a professor of theology at Saint John's Seminary in Camarillo, California. He is the author or editor of more than twenty books, including *The Heart of Hope* (2005), and recipient of several honorary doctorates.

Roberto Escamilla is the author of *Prisoners of Hope: Essays on Life's Journey* (The Upper Room, 1981).

Andrew Greeley, priest, sociologist, author, and journalist, is a professor of sociology at the University of Arizona and a research associate with the National Opinion Research Center at the University of Chicago. He is the author of more than fifty best-selling novels and more than 100 works of nonfiction.

Stanley Hauerwas is a professor who studies the importance of the church as well as narrative for understanding Christian existence. Named "America's Best Theologian" by *Time* magazine in 2001, Dr. Hauerwas holds a joint appointment at Duke Divinity School and Duke University School of Law.

E. Glenn Hinson is professor emeritus of church spirituality and history at Baptist Theological Seminary at Richmond. He has authored numerous books, articles, essays, and reviews.

John Indermark, a native of Saint Louis, lives in southwest Washington with his wife, Judy. He is an ordained minister in the United Church of Christ and his titles for Upper Room Books include *Neglected Voices*, *Traveling the Prayer Paths of Jesus*, *Turn Toward Promise*, *Parables and Passion*, *Genesis of Grace*, and *Setting the Christmas Stage*.

Rueben P. Job is a retired United Methodist bishop and former World Editor and Publisher of The Upper Room. His titles for Upper Room Books include *A Guide to Prayer for Ministers and Other Servants*, *A Guide to Prayer for All God's People*, *A Guide to Prayer for All Who Seek God*, and *Spiritual Life in the Congregation*.

Martin Luther (1483–1546), a priest and professor of theology who initiated the Protestant Reformation.

Martin E. Marty has authored more than fifty books, including a National Book Award winner. He is an ordained minister and has taught at the University of Chicago for more than thirty-five years.

Leigh McLeroy writes and speaks with a passion for God and a keen eye for God's presence in everyday life. In addition to *The Sacred Ordinary*, she is the author of *The Beautiful Ache* (Baker/Revell, 2007).

Parker J. Palmer is a writer and traveling teacher who works independently on issues in spirituality, community, education, leadership, and social change. His books include *The Company of Strangers*, *To Know as We Are Known*, *The Active Life*, *Let Your Life Speak*, and *The Courage to Teach*.

Robbie Clifton Pinter is an English professor at Belmont University in Nashville, Tennessee, where she also serves as a spiritual director. Her other writing includes *For This Child I Prayed* (Cold Tree, 2004).

Jim Wallis is editor-in-chief/chief executive officer of *Sojourners* magazine.

Amy Lyles Wilson is a writer, editor, and workshop leader in Nashville, Tennessee. A graduate of Vanderbilt University Divinity School, her byline has appeared in a variety of publications, including *This I Believe II: More Personal Philosophies of Remarkable Men and Women* (Henry Holt, 2008) and *Her Nashville* (www.hernashville.com).

Miriam Thérèse Winter, Ph.D., is a Medical Mission Sister and Professor of Liturgy, Worship, Spirituality, and Feminist Studies at Hartford Seminary, Hartford, Connecticut. Her published works include *The Singer and the Song*, *WomanWisdom*, and *The Gospel According to Mary*.

Andrew Greeley, *Death and Beyond* © 1976 by the Thomas More Association, Chicago, Illinois. Used by permission of the author.

Stanley Hauerwas, *A Community of Character: Toward a Constructive Christian Social Ethic*, copyright © 1981 by University of Notre Dame Press.

E. Glenn Hinson, "Suffering and Hope," *Weavings: A Journal of the Christian Spiritual Life* 18, no. 4 (July/August 2003): 13. Used by permission of the author.

"Hope," from *The Upper Room Dictionary of Christian Spiritual Formation* © 2003 by Upper Room Books. Used by permission.

John Indermark, *Hope: Our Longing for Home*, copyright © 2007 by John Indermark. Used by permission of Upper Room Books.

Rueben P. Job, *A Guide to Prayer for All Who Seek God*, copyright © 2003 by Norman Shawchuck and Rueben P. Job. Used by permission of Upper Room Books.

Leigh McLeroy, "No Hope—or New Hope?," *The Sacred Ordinary: Embracing the Holy in the Everyday*, published by Revell, a division of Baker Publishing Group © 2008. Used by permission.

Martin E. Marty, *Our Hope for Years to Come: The Search for Spiritual Sanctuary* (Minneapolis, MN: Augsburg Fortress, 1995), 83.

Parker J. Palmer, *Let Your Life Speak: Listening for the Voice of Vocation*, copyright © 2000 by Jossey-Bass, Inc. Reprinted with permission of John Wiley & Sons, Inc.

Robbie Clifton Pinter, "The Landscape Listens," *Alive Now* (January/February 2004): 6–10. Used by permission of the author.

Paragraph from p. 347: "Perhaps the only people ... decision for hope" from GOD'S POLITICS: WHY THE RIGHT GETS IT WRONG AND THE LEFT DOESN'T GET IT by JIM WALLIS. Copyright © 2005 by Jim Wallis. Reprinted by permission of HarperCollins Publishers.

Poem by Miriam Thérèse Winter as reprinted in *Women Pray: Voices through the Ages, from Many Faiths, Cultures, and Traditions* © 2001 by Monica Furlong. Permission granted by SkyLight Paths Publishing, P. O. Box 237, Woodstock, VT 05091. www.skylightpaths.com